BRINK OF EXTINCTION

CAN WE STOP NATURE'S DECLINE?

by Eric Braun

Consultant:
Sanya Carley, PhD
O'Neill School of Public and Environmental Affairs
Indiana University

COMPASS POINT BOOKS
a capstone imprint

Informed! is published by Compass Point Books, an imprint of Capstone.
1710 Roe Crest Drive
North Mankato, Minnesota 56003
www.capstonepub.com

Library of Congress Cataloging-in-Publication Data is available on the Library of Congress website.
ISBN: 978-0-7565-6619-7 (hardcover)
ISBN: 978-0-7565-6663-0 (paperback)
ISBN: 978-0-7565-6627-2 (ebook PDF)

Summary: An intergovernmental science agency recently concluded that one million species, plants, and animals are at risk of extinction because of nature's dangerous decline. What is the cause of this decline? And what are humans doing to protect themselves and other species? Readers will discover the facts behind this issue, the interconnectedness of species on Earth, and the immediate action needed to address the rapid loss of biodiversity.

Image Credits
Alamy: Chronicle, 40; Getty Images: Antonio RIBEIRO, 18, Stringer, 28; iStockphoto: DurkTalsma, 22, PocholoCalapre, 12; National Archives and Records Administration: 27; Newscom: Stock Connection Worldwide/Loren McIntyre, 5, UPI/Jemal Countess, 52; Science Source: Biophoto Associates, 21, Mike Agliolo, 37, MSF/Raúl Martín, 38; Shutterstock: Aaron Schwartz, 46, Alex Farias, 6, Belovodchenko Anton, 32, COMEO/Frederic Legrand, 19, Gudkov Andrey, 45, Jack Bell Photography, 9, Jason Grant, 26, John A. Anderson, 34, Joseph Sorrentino, 33, Kent Weakley, 15, Melissa King, 16, Mikadun, 8, Milan Zygmunt, 41, PHOTOOBJECT, 44, Phrompas, 51, Rachael Warriner, 48, Richard Whitcombe, 7, Scott F Smith, 20, Sergei Bachlakov, 50, Solid Photos, 10, Sumruay Rattanataipob, 13, Tapui, 24, TJmedia, 4, 20 (top), 34 (top), 47, 59, Underawesternsky, 43, Vlad Siaber, 25, Volodymyr Burdiak, cover; Wikimedia: Public Domain, 42

Editorial Credits
Designer: Kay Fraser; Media Researcher: Eric Gohl; Production Specialist: Kathy McColley

Printed and bound in the USA
PA117

TABLE OF CONTENTS

CHAPTER 1

A PLANET IN CRISIS

In summer 2019, media outlets began reporting on fires ravaging the Amazon rain forest. Huge sections of one of Earth's most critical habitats were ablaze, filling the sky with a choking black smoke that caused darkness to fall hours before sunset in São Paulo, Brazil. By the end of August, the Amazon had experienced nearly 40,000 fires that year.

The Amazon rain forest, 60 percent of which is in Brazil, is home to an incredible number of living species. At least 40,000 plant species and more than 400 types of mammals live there. So do about 1,300 bird, 2,200 fish, 378 reptile, 428 amphibian, and at least 96,000 invertebrate species. And let's not forget the 2.5 million insect species. About 10 percent of the known species on Earth make the Amazon their home. When the forest disappears, their habitat disappears.

Forest fires are common in the Amazon rain forest during the dry season—July to October. Many are caused by natural events, such as lightning strikes, but the 2019 fires were largely caused by humans clearing the land for farming.

Among the most important living organisms in the Amazon are its trees. The forest has billions of them, divided into about 16,000 species. The Amazon's trees are critical to Earth's health because they remove huge amounts of carbon dioxide from the atmosphere during the photosynthesis process. Carbon dioxide is the gas that's warming the planet. During photosynthesis, the trees convert the carbon in the gas to sugar, which they store and use as food. Fewer trees mean more carbon dioxide in the atmosphere and faster warming. The Amazon's trees also produce 6 percent of the world's oxygen, which is released into the atmosphere as a by-product of photosynthesis. Most living things need oxygen to survive.

Shockingly, the Amazon fires didn't happen by accident. Someone lit them. Research indicates that humans start 99 percent of all fires in the Amazon. Why, when Earth depends on the rain forest for so much, would people do that? Brazil's president, Jair Bolsonaro, supports opening the Amazon to farming, ranching, and other economic development. On August 10, 2019, farmers and ranchers near the town of Novo Progresso set fires on their land in support of Bolsonaro's policies. That day, the government recorded 124 fires in the area.

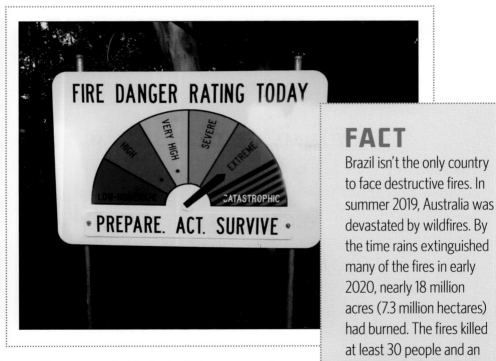

Signs are posted in Australia to warn people about the daily risks of fire and cautioning them to act responsibly.

FACT

Brazil isn't the only country to face destructive fires. In summer 2019, Australia was devastated by wildfires. By the time rains extinguished many of the fires in early 2020, nearly 18 million acres (7.3 million hectares) had burned. The fires killed at least 30 people and an estimated 1 billion animals.

If the climate change causing coral to become bleached is prolonged, the coral eventually dies.

Human Impact

The burning of the Amazon is just one dramatic example of the many ways that humans are contributing to the decrease of plant and animal species. But our impact can be seen in countless ways throughout Earth.

Consider the bleaching of coral reefs, such as the famous Great Barrier Reef off the coast of Australia. This once-colorful reef has evolved during hundreds of millions of years to form a vast, diverse ecosystem. But as human-caused climate change has led to rising ocean temperatures, this reef and others like it are being drained of color and are turning brittle.

Like rain forests, reefs are home to countless species of plants and animals. In addition to the 4,000 fish species and 800 species of corals, scientists estimate that reefs are a habitat for 1 million to 8 million species of organisms that have yet to be discovered. In addition to supporting all that life, reefs also prevent land erosion and protect wetlands, ports, and harbors in coastal communities from waves and storms. And they support these communities' economies by providing fisheries and tourism.

It's not just warming that is damaging the reefs. Other human-created causes include sewage and pollution. Litter, oil and chemical spills, sediment from construction, and other toxins run off the land. If things don't change, the world will lose 99 percent of its coral reefs in the next few decades.

"It will be like lots of lights blinking off," scientist David Obura said of the colorful reefs disappearing bit by bit. Obura is chair of the Coral Specialist Group in the International Union for Conservation of Nature (IUCN). This global association of government and private organizations works to understand and preserve

Mine drainage is high in metals and minerals and can contaminate drinking water, disrupt aquatic plants and animals, and corrode structures such as bridges.

the natural world. Obura went on to say that the next generation of children won't have the chance to see coral reefs—because they won't exist. "In five decades we have undermined the global climate so fundamentally that in the next generation we will lose the globally connected reef system that has survived tens of millions of years."

Closer to Home

For most of us the Amazon rain forest is far away, so we might not strongly feel its loss. Likewise, few people have been lucky enough to see the underwater beauty of a coral reef. For a more familiar example, though, look to the skies and trees near your own home.

A report from Cornell University in New York said that North America has lost about one-third of all wild birds since the 1970s. That's nearly 3 billion birds that have disappeared during the past 50 years, in every biome from forests to grasslands. The song of the western meadowlark, which used to be a loud and common choir

Western meadowlark

in midwestern fields, has grown quieter as its population dropped 1 percent every year since 1970. The population of green herons has declined by half since then. About 25 percent of blue jays are gone.

The causes of these losses, like those of the Amazon fires and the bleached coral reefs, can be traced to humans. Destroying habitats deprives birds of safe breeding grounds. Introducing invasive plant species drives out native plants that birds need for food. And pesticides kill about 67 million birds each year.

Human activity is taking a huge toll on biodiversity, which is the variety of life on Earth. The biggest influence on declining biodiversity is changes in land use. That includes habitat destruction—practices such as converting

FACT
Earth has lost at least 680 vertebrate species during the last few hundred years. Scientists estimate that the world may be losing dozens of species every day.

A combine harvested wheat and poured it into a trailer. Approximately three-fourths of all U.S. grain products are made from wheat flour.

natural habitats for agriculture, developing land for towns and cities, and mountaintop mining. People have altered more than 75 percent of Earth's land, turning it into farm fields, ranches, roads, and concrete cityscapes. Since the 1700s, we've drained about 85 percent of the world's wetlands, which are ecosystems in flooded areas with aquatic plants and vegetation.

FOREST ELEPHANTS

Somewhere deep in the rain forest in the Republic of the Congo, Africa, a forest elephant munches on a small softwood tree. As the elephant stomps around, it smashes small trees and bushes beneath its feet. All around it, much taller, older trees tower toward the sky.

This elephant doesn't know it, but it's playing an important role in conserving life on Earth. Forest elephants, which are much smaller than the savanna elephants that live in grasslands, eat and stomp smaller trees that grow on the rain forest floor. In doing so, the elephants clear space to allow more light to reach the forest. With fewer small trees competing for water and nutrients, the larger trees have more resources to grow. Those large, slow-growing hardwood trees store much more carbon than smaller trees and plants. By clearing the small trees, forest elephants promote the growth of carbon-storing large trees.

But these forest elephants are in danger of extinction due to poaching, or illegal hunting. Elephants are protected from hunting by law, but many people disobey the law so they can sell the elephants' ivory tusks, which are prized for ornaments and jewelry. Scientists estimate that central

Africa's rain forests will lose about 3 billion tons (2.7 billion metric tons) of carbon if its forest elephants die off. That's almost as much carbon dioxide as the country of France emits over the course of 27 years!

Other Human Causes

Humans also contribute to the loss of biodiversity in other ways. We burn fossil fuels to heat our homes and power our cars. The by-products of these fuels are a primary cause of global climate change. We also cause pollution by dumping sewage, fertilizers, and chemicals into waterways. Even noise pollution from cities and industrial activity can affect animals and marine life.

Resource exploitation is another major factor in the loss of biodiversity. Humans use a lot of resources. We hunt and fish for food. We cut down trees for wood. We use water for farming and raising animals. Those actions leave fewer resources for other living things on the planet.

The introduction of invasive species is a problem too. When we move plants or animals from their native habitat into another habitat, it can upset the ecological balance in the new habitat. For example, non-native buckthorn crowds out native plants in Minnesota. The insects that feed on the lost native plants are left with less food. As a result, the insect population declines, leaving the birds that feed on those insects with less to eat. In turn, this affects the animals that prey on the birds.

The monarch butterfly population is struggling because its primary food, the milkweed plant, is in decline.

The results of these activities are dramatic. Some tropical forests are silent because the insects are gone. We're losing soil so quickly that land is turning to desert in many areas. The number of native species in land-based habitats has decreased by an average of 20 percent since

1900. Forested areas fell by 7 percent just between 2000 and 2013.

What about the oceans? We've affected about 66 percent of Earth's marine environment through shipping, underwater mining, fish farms, and other actions. In parts of the oceans, there's no longer enough oxygen to support life. There are at least 400 of these areas, known as dead zones, where there's nothing but green slime. Put them all together, and you'd have a dead zone that is bigger than the state of Wyoming.

Worldwide, about 1 million species are at risk of extinction.

It's Getting Crowded

FACT
A recent study found that more than 40 percent of insect species are declining and one-third are endangered. They could disappear within 100 years.

At the root of all this species destruction is a simple fact—two things can't be in the same place at the same time. As humans reproduce, the world population grows. The more people on Earth, the less space there is for other living things. Experts estimate that there were about 50 million people on Earth in 1000 BC. By AD 1700, there were about 600 million, meaning it took about 2,700 years for the population to grow by 650 million. The world population in 1900 was 1.6 *billion*. It's only grown more quickly since then. In 2019, about 7.7 billion people lived on Earth. By 2050, it's estimated the population will grow to 9.7 billion.

There are nearly 140 million housing units in the United States.

World Population Through Time

In July 2019, the world population hit almost 7.6 billion. It is projected to hit 9.5 billion before 2050.

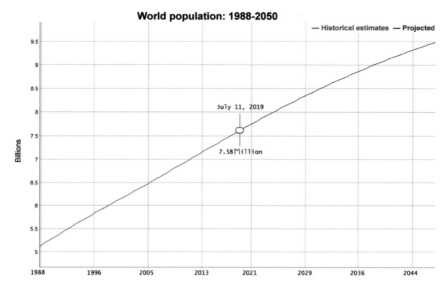

World population: 1988-2050

— Historical estimates — Projected

July 11, 2019

7.58 Million

More people means that more land is used to support human activity. Even if we treat that land well, which often isn't the case, less land is available for other species.

The fires lit in the Amazon to clear land for economic development are a symbol of what humans have done to biodiversity. We can put out the fires. Maybe we can save the Amazon. But the bigger picture is more alarming. We can't stop taking up space. We can't stop using resources. So what can we do?

The truth is that there are many things we can do to reverse the trend of declining biodiversity. It helps to understand the answer to a basic question: Why should we even care about biodiversity?

In 2018, Americans spent $47.8 billion on lawn and garden products.

The answer is complicated but also simple—because all life on Earth, including human life, is interconnected and interdependent. The dangers of global warming and declining biodiversity have been clear for generations, but there's been little political effort to do anything about it. Big changes can feel risky, and the benefits aren't easy to accept. Fossil fuels make lots of money for many people, so it can be worrisome for those people to think about using less of them. A rancher can't always see the benefits that forests provide the world, but cutting down forests to raise cattle can put money into a bank account. A homeowner might be aware that lawn fertilizer is bad for the environment, but it's difficult to understand why it's bad when it makes the lawn lush and weed-free.

A Treaty to Save Biodiversity

In June 1992, the United Nations hosted the first Earth Summit in Rio de Janeiro, Brazil. At the summit, 168 nations signed the Convention on Biological Diversity (CBD), a treaty with an overall goal of conserving the world's biodiversity. Also, 154 countries signed an agreement acknowledging the threat of global warming and agreeing to reduce greenhouse gas emissions. The number of signed nations has since grown to 197, and representatives from these countries have continued to meet every year. It eventually became clear, however, that the nations' efforts weren't enough to keep Earth from warming 3.6 degrees Fahrenheit (2 degrees Celsius)

Children celebrated at the United Nations Conference on Environment and Development, also known as the Rio de Janeiro Earth Summit, in June 1992.

compared to pre-industrial levels—the goal they had established for reducing the dangerous impacts of climate change.

In 2015 the nations met in Paris, France, and adopted the Paris Agreement, which included more rigorous requirements and goals. The agreement encourages countries to divest from fossil fuels and reduce greenhouse gas emissions. A specific guideline is the 20/20/20 targets, which involve reducing carbon dioxide emissions by 20 percent, increasing the market share of renewable energies to 20 percent, and increasing energy efficiency by 20 percent.

However, the Paris Agreement lacks strength because it doesn't include a legal way to force countries to meet any specified compliance level. Nations set their own standards and report to other nations. But if a nation doesn't set strong standards or meet the standards it does set, the rest of the world has no real recourse. And in April 2019 the Paris Agreement received a major blow when President Donald Trump began the process to legally withdraw the United States from the agreement.

President Barack Obama delivered a speech at the 2015 United Nations Climate Change Conference in Paris.

CHAPTER 2

THE WEB OF LIFE

Step outside and you'll likely see countless forms of life. You might see trees, grass, shrubs, and flowers. You may hear birds singing or see them soaring through the air. Squirrels, chipmunks, mice, and other rodents are common, not to mention many insects.

Go a little farther from home, such as to a park or nature preserve, and the count increases. Long-legged great blue herons stand in the shallow areas of a pond. Beavers swim toward their dens. Fish, crayfish, lampreys, and bacteria live in the water.

Great blue heron

Mosses and lichen cling to logs or rocks. And yes, there are plenty of bugs.

Of course, you could sit in the park counting life-forms all day and night, and you'd never come close to seeing them all. A recent study by researchers from the University of Arizona estimates that the world is home to about 2 billion living species. Plants, animals, and other living things are the planet's valuable assets. Together with the land, water, and air, they form the ecosystems where we live.

FACT
Between 70 and 90 percent of living species are bacteria.

Life Is Linked

Before we had the data and knowledge that we do now, it was possible to think of protecting nature as something we should do for its own sake. It might have seemed like the right thing to do to prevent species from going extinct. But now we know that species richness and diversity are directly linked to our own lives. A biodiversity crisis is a threat to our health and our way of life. Biodiversity is critical to regulating the climate; controlling floods and other natural disasters; protecting coasts from erosion and damage; and providing us with food, fresh water, medicines, fuel, building materials, and air.

The relationship between climate change and declining biodiversity is circular. Climate change contributes to declining biodiversity as rising temperatures make habitats less livable for all sorts of species. Species begin to die out, including plants that store carbon dioxide. Warmer oceans are less capable of storing carbon. Less carbon being stored in plants and the ocean means more carbon in the atmosphere. And in turn, more carbon in the atmosphere leads to rising temperatures.

Ice calving—chunks of ice breaking off glaciers—is becoming more common in Arctic and Antarctic regions as global temperatures rise.

Global warming contributes to melting of the glaciers and Arctic sea ice, which has a negative effect on humans. For example, about one-sixth of the world's people depend on glaciers and snowmelt for their fresh water supply.

As glaciers disappear, so does the fresh water they provide. Melting also causes sea levels to rise, which threatens coastal communities with flooding.

A Changing World

Extreme weather due to global warming is already more common. Our hottest days are hotter, and our coldest days are colder. Severe weather events such as deadly heat waves, hurricanes, and tornadoes occur more often and are projected to continue to increase.

Mangroves are woody trees or shrubs that grow along coasts and in swamps. With their tangle of roots and dense branches, they form a barrier that protects coasts from storms such as hurricanes. Coral reefs do the same thing. When mangroves and coral reefs die out, they expose coastal communities to flooding and dangerous waves. Scientists estimate that the loss of mangroves and coral reefs will put the homes of as many as 300 million people at an increased risk of flood damage.

Wetlands are critical areas that store carbon and reduce flooding by absorbing heavy rainfall. They purify water by absorbing chemicals, filtering out pollution, and counteracting harmful bacteria. But today, less than 15 percent of wetlands exist compared to 300 years ago. More than 50 percent of the world's wetlands have disappeared since 1900, mainly due to human activity.

Forests also play an important role in purifying water. That's because forests help prevent erosion and reduce the

Mangrove restoration projects are underway in many areas to try to reduce coastal erosion.

risk of landslides that can contaminate water supplies. Trees can filter out pollutants such as pesticides. About one-third of the world's largest cities depend on protected forests for at least part of their water supply.

Besides water, humans depend heavily on biodiversity for other important resources. For example, many medicines are made from plants. In the Western Hemisphere, about 25 percent of prescription drugs contain ingredients that come from plants. Medicines derived from plants treat a huge variety of ailments, including cancer, pain, and cold symptoms. Traditional medicine, which often includes plant, animal, and mineral sources, also relies on a variety of species. Worldwide, people harvest between 50,000 and 70,000 plant species for Western and traditional medicine.

What's for Dinner?

What about food? In many countries, especially those with high levels of poverty, people depend on meat from wild animals. Worldwide, we take about 110 million tons (100 million metric tons) of aquatic life from the wild, including fish and other seafood. When species decline, there's less of those resources available. Loss of biodiversity also leads to land degradation, making the land less suitable to grow food.

FACT

According to the U.S. Department of Agriculture (USDA), bee pollination is responsible for one out of every four bites of food you eat every day!

Bees are perhaps the most important insects on Earth. The 20,000 known species of bees play a huge role in human survival. They pollinate about 75 percent of the fruits, vegetables, and nuts grown in the United States, allowing them to produce fruit. If bees and other pollinating insects and animals disappear, plants won't be pollinated. Without pollination, plants can't produce food for humans and animals.

The varieties of plants and animals that humans rely on to produce food have been decreasing dramatically. We have domesticated nearly 8,000 mammal breeds for use in agriculture. Of those, 26 percent are in danger of extinction. People also have raised more than 6,000 plant species for food. But of these species, just nine make up 66 percent of all crops worldwide.

Food production is part of another cycle. As declining biodiversity and global warming make it harder to grow produce or raise livestock, agriculture itself makes climate change worse. In some parts of the world, such as Indonesia and Malaysia, farmers drain wetlands to grow crops or raise livestock. In other areas, such as the Amazon, forests are burned to make grazing land for livestock.

FACT

When taking into account the water required to care for cattle, it takes an estimated 460 gallons (1,741 liters) of water to make one quarter-pound (0.1 kilogram) hamburger.

Money Matters

If maintaining healthy food and water, a clean environment, and an adequate supply of food and medicine isn't enough reason to worry about declining biodiversity, the International Union for Conservation of Nature (IUCN) has another way to understand the problem. It calculated the monetary value of goods and services that Earth's ecosystems provide. That number is $33 trillion each year. To put it in context, the 2017 U.S. gross domestic product (GDP), which is the total monetary value of all goods and services produced in the country, was more than $19 trillion.

Among the many soup kitchens set up during the Great Depression was one funded by gangster Al Capone because he "couldn't stand it to see those poor devils starving."

Research suggests that if global warming continues, there's a greater than 50 percent chance that global GDP will drop by 20 percent by the end of this century. By comparison, the Great Depression (1929–1939) saw a decline of about 15 percent. In other words, much of the world would be plunged into poverty. And while the world was able to recover from the Great Depression, these environmental losses would likely be permanent.

Of course, the most important and immediate value of biodiversity isn't measured in dollars. Instead, it's measured in our own survival and well-being. Marine ecologist and National Geographic Explorer-in-Residence Enric Sala put it this way, "Every morsel of food, every sip of water, the air we breathe is the result of work done by other species. Nature gives us everything we need to survive." Speaking about the world's living species, he added, "Without them, there is no us."

Syrian farmers worked the drought-ridden land in the Hasaka region in 2010.

WATER WARS AND REFUGEES

Declining biodiversity and global climate change have indirectly led to violence and refugee crises. It starts with their effect on weather and resources, and most of it can be traced back to water.

One example of a water crisis was in Syria, which experienced a drought that began in 2006 and lasted five years. Without enough water, crops failed. The food shortage was a major factor in the political chaos and subsequent civil war in the country. Since 2011, more than 5 million people have fled Syria to seek safety in other countries.

In Africa, about 393,000 people are expected to die in battle by 2030 as a direct result of rising temperatures. Climate-caused violence and instability are expected to spike the number of refugees fleeing sub-Saharan Africa, Latin America, and South Asia.

The World Bank is an international organization that funds and supports its member countries in efforts to reduce poverty and improve living standards for low-income people. It estimates that climate changes will force 140 million refugees to leave their countries by 2050. The United Nations (UN), an international organization of countries dedicated to maintaining international peace and security, projects an even larger number. The UN puts the likely total at 200 million, but possibly as many as 1 billion or more—as the report says, "a billion or more vulnerable poor people with little choice but to fight or flee."

Water and climate expert Peter Gleick compiled a list of all armed conflicts since 3000 BC that stemmed from water issues. The list has more than 500 entries, more than half of which have occurred since 2010. While Gleick acknowledges that part of the reason for that number is that there's more data available in recent history, it's still a remarkable finding. "There's a saying in the water community," Gleick said. "If climate change is a shark, the water resources are the teeth."

A Blueprint for Change

In spring 2019 the Intergovernmental Science-Policy Platform on Biodiversity and Ecosystem Services (IPBES) released a report detailing the effects of declining biodiversity. The IPBES is an intergovernmental body formed to strengthen the relationship between science and policy to better preserve biodiversity and ecosystems. Its report was compiled by 145 expert authors from 50 countries. In order to turn back these trends, the report said the world needs to make transformative changes.

"We are eroding the very foundations of economies, livelihoods, food security, health, and quality of life worldwide," said IPBES chair Robert Watson. "We have lost time. We must act now."

The IPBES report points out that "global goals for conserving and sustainably using nature and achieving sustainability cannot be met" if we keep our efforts at the same rate they are now. Good progress has been made on only four of the 20 Aichi Biodiversity Targets. Most targets likely won't be achieved by the deadline.

Aichi Biodiversity Targets

In 2010 the signing nations agreed to 20 biodiversity targets—known as the Aichi Biodiversity Targets—to be met by 2020. The targets are grouped into five strategic goals:

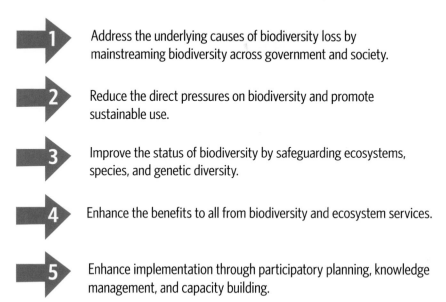

1 Address the underlying causes of biodiversity loss by mainstreaming biodiversity across government and society.

2 Reduce the direct pressures on biodiversity and promote sustainable use.

3 Improve the status of biodiversity by safeguarding ecosystems, species, and genetic diversity.

4 Enhance the benefits to all from biodiversity and ecosystem services.

5 Enhance implementation through participatory planning, knowledge management, and capacity building.

Credit: Convention on Biological Diversity, www.cbd.int/sp/targets

Studies in 2017 pointed out that none of the major industrialized nations were implementing the policies they had set for themselves. None had met their targets for reducing emissions. Even if the nations had met the targets, the study's authors projected that Earth would still warm by 5.4°F (3°C). A 2018 report indicated that Earth could warm by as much as 7.2°F (4°C) or even 9°F (5°C) degrees.

But change is possible. The IPBES report authors say it all comes down to being more efficient with our resources. Farmers and ranchers can learn to produce more food on less land. One way to do that is by producing less beef and

Unregulated discharges from factories or sewage treatment facilities can result in water pollution and unsafe drinking water. Some of the chemicals discharged are harmless, but others are toxic to people and wildlife.

lamb, which use more resources than other animals raised for food, such as hogs or poultry. People need to waste less food, and everyone needs to use natural resources more efficiently. Governments must monitor and punish illegal logging, hunting, and fishing, as well as pollutants such as heavy metals and untreated wastewater.

The report provides ideas to increase sustainability in agriculture, forestry, marine systems, freshwater systems, urban areas, energy, and finance. Most importantly, it emphasizes the importance of cooperation between industries and between nations. A key factor is for worldwide financial and economic systems to focus on a sustainable economy as well as economic growth.

The authors of the report also stress that indigenous peoples—ethnic groups who are original inhabitants of a region—should play an important part in the process moving forward. Declining biodiversity and global climate

Coffee is one of Mexico's most profitable exports. Nearly half a million small farmers and their families rely on coffee bean crops for their economic survival.

change are projected to have major negative impacts on the areas where indigenous peoples live. Yet plans to solve these issues often don't consider indigenous peoples' ideas, perspectives, rights, or values. These groups have innovations and practices, such as crop rotation, that would be both helpful and fair in solving these problems. Another example of indigenous agricultural practice is agroforestry, the maintenance and planting of trees to develop a microclimate that protects crops against temperature extremes.

CHAPTER 3

THE GREAT EXTINCTIONS

Earth formed about 4.5 billion years ago, and its oceans appeared about 3.8 billion years ago. Life-forms appeared between 4.29 and 3.7 billion years ago. They were likely a form of bacteria that received energy from the sun and made food through photosynthesis. Eventually, single-cell organisms began to cluster together. About 800 million years ago, these clusters became the world's first animals. By about 580 million years ago, a variety of creatures lived on the ocean floor. Since then, the richness and abundance of life on Earth has grown.

FACT

Sponges were among the first animals on Earth.

Mass Extinctions Throughout History

End Ordovician

suspected cause: dramatic fluctuations in sea level

result: sea creatures drastically reduced

Late Devonian

suspected causes: asteroid impact; global cooling; loss of oxygen in oceans

result: 75% species extinction

End Permian (The Great Dying)

suspected causes: climate and sea level fluctuation; asteroid impacts; volcanoes

result: 96% species extinction

End Triassic

suspected causes: global warming; volcanoes

result: 70-75% species extinction

End Cretaceous

suspected causes: asteroid impact and volcanoes

result: death of dinosaurs

485

383

252

201

66

Millions of Years Ago (start dates of extinctions)

At times, though, it has also contracted. Large extinction events have dramatically reduced the diversity of life on Earth. Of those extinctions, five are labeled the "Big Five" because their effect was so great. The first one was called the End Ordovician Extinction and wiped out about 80 percent of life. The most recent great extinction started about 66 million years ago at the end of the Cretaceous period. That's the event that killed 50 to 75 percent of all species on the planet, including the dinosaurs. Scientists now generally agree that a meteor that hit near the Yucatán Peninsula off the coast of Mexico caused this event.

THE GREAT DYING

The worst great extinction in Earth's history happened about 252 million years ago, marking the end of the Permian geologic period. This event is known as "The Great Dying." One of its causes was a volcanic eruption near Siberia that belched carbon dioxide into the atmosphere, warming it by about 9°F (5°C). That triggered a release of the flammable gas methane, which warmed the atmosphere even more.

The warming caused oceans to lose about 80 percent of their oxygen. Without oxygen, the oceans were unable to support life, killing about 96 percent of marine species. It wasn't much better for animals on land. About 70 percent of land species were lost. It took Earth millions of years to recover from the Permian extinction event.

In addition to other factors, scientists believe a large impact on Earth from an asteroid or comet led to the extinction of dinosaurs, as depicted in this artistic rendering.

A Whole New World

Mass extinctions change Earth's character because it takes millions of years to recover from them. And when it does recover, it usually looks very different. For example, the Cretaceous period had only a few species of mammals and an abundance of dinosaurs. After the extinction event, the dinosaurs were gone, and mammals eventually took over.

Recent findings show that early humans hunting woolly mammoths was the main cause of the species' extinction.

That brings us to today, a time when biologists generally agree that we are in the midst of a new mass-extinction event. If current trends hold, Earth will lose at least half of its species by 2100. However, this extinction is different. Volcanic eruptions, asteroid strikes, and natural climate shifts caused previous extinctions. The sixth extinction isn't being caused by any accidental or sudden event. Instead, people's actions are the main cause.

Homo sapiens didn't appear on Earth until about 200,000 years ago. These early people first appeared in a small part of eastern Africa, but they soon spread to other areas. Everywhere they went, they left their mark. They hunted mammals on land and gathered shellfish along the coast. They found creatures, such as pig-size hippos and giant lizards, that didn't have the capacity to live in harmony with humans. Many of these species soon died out, a casualty of meeting humans.

Humans continued to spread throughout the world, and they continued to alter it. They cut down forests to grow food. They rerouted streams and rivers. Shortly after people arrived in Australia, animals such as land tortoises the size of small cars began to disappear. After people arrived in North America, large mammals such as saber-toothed tigers and mammoths went extinct. The same thing happened in South America, where dozens of species of large mammals started dying out. As humans moved into new areas, the pattern repeated itself. More species disappeared.

Causes of these changes included people hunting animals to extinction, overfishing, and spreading invasive species from one area to another. One of the biggest causes was people altering the landscape. No other species has altered Earth as much as humans have.

Fueling the Problem

As early as 1000 BC, humans discovered fossil fuels such as coal and began to burn them for warmth. This process changed Earth's atmosphere, especially after the Industrial Revolution began in the mid-1700s. Coal became the primary source of energy. It changed the oceans'

People proudly sent postcards of a 1930 view of Staffordshire, England, believing that the factory smog symbolized success and prosperity in their town.

chemistry, as well as the world's climate. Many species of plants and animals died out.

An example is amphibians, which appeared about 400 million years ago. Early frogs and toads appeared about 250 million years ago. That means amphibians have survived four of the five great extinctions, and frogs and toads specifically have survived two. Amphibians are hardy. They know how to survive.

Yet in the 1980s, scientists began to notice that it was harder to find frogs, toads, and other amphibians. At first there was controversy about what was happening. Were amphibians really declining, or was it just a random variation? But eventually it was clear that amphibians were dying out. Today, more than 40 percent of amphibians are threatened with extinction.

What happened? Many things affect amphibians, including habitat destruction and pollution. But the most important factor turned out to be a chytrid fungi called

A fungus found naturally on African clawed frogs is believed to be responsible for the decline in global frog populations.

Batrachochytrium dendrobatidis, or Bd for short. Bd was found on dead frogs throughout the world. Through testing, scientists discovered that Bd would kill many frog species within weeks.

In 2004 Australian pathologist Rick Speare discovered that Bd was present on African clawed frogs, but the fungus didn't harm them. This frog species always had Bd on them. However, in the 1930s, scientists had discovered that African clawed frogs could be used to test for pregnancy in human women. People began to ship these frogs out of their native habitat to doctors' offices all over the world, spreading Bd with them. Maybe a few of those frogs got loose and found a home in the wild. Or perhaps water from their tanks was poured into habitats where other frogs lived. Whatever the case, Bd began to spread slowly but surely. And frog populations began to plummet.

According to recent research, introducing non-native species into new habitats is one of the five main factors causing the sixth great extinction. The other causes are changes in land and sea use, direct exploitation of organisms, climate change, and pollution. All of these factors can be traced to humans.

Self-Destruction

What's alarming about the sixth extinction isn't just that we're doing it to ourselves, but how fast we're doing it. One of the five great extinction events was the End Permian, or Permian-Triassic, extinction about 252 million years ago. Carbon dioxide entering the atmosphere and spiking global temperatures caused that event. Today we are adding carbon to the atmosphere at least ten times faster. In the past 100 years, carbon dioxide levels in the atmosphere have changed as much as they normally do in a 100,000-year glacial cycle.

Svante Arrhenius

People have known about the threat from global warming long enough to do something about it. In 1896 Swedish scientist Svante Arrhenius was the first to publish his theory about the greenhouse effect, in which added carbon dioxide in the atmosphere traps heat and raises the global temperature. American scientist Charles Keeling proved the theory in 1960. By the early 1970s, many members of the scientific community were anxious about climate change. In 1975 the first article that used the phrase *global warming* was published.

Many people became concerned, but it wasn't until June 23, 1988, that a true alarm bell sounded. That was the day climate scientist James E. Hansen testified before the U.S. Senate. Hansen's message was clear: "The greenhouse effect has been detected and is changing our climate now." Coincidentally, that was right around the same time that other scientists were discovering the disappearance of certain species of frogs.

Recent Changes

We've actually done more damage to the planet's ability to sustain life in the years since that Senate testimony than we did in all of human history before it. More than half of the carbon that we've released into the atmosphere from

There are 567 national wildlife refuges in the United States.

burning fossil fuels has been in the last 30 or so years. Globally, we now extract approximately 60 billion tons of renewable and nonrenewable resources every year, a number that has nearly doubled since 1980. Greenhouse gases have doubled since 1980. Urban population areas have more than doubled since 1992. Species may be going extinct hundreds of times faster than historic rates. If current trends continue, life on Earth will likely include water shortages, food shortages, climate instability, and widespread poverty and violence. Even human survival may be at risk.

Forty years ago, bald eagles were in danger of extinction. Now they no longer need Endangered Species Act protection because their population is healthy and growing.

But there is hope. Scientists at zoos, laboratories, and research outposts have put incredible efforts into rescuing dying species. They're often quite successful.

Many protected areas such as nature preserves have been established throughout the world to safeguard habitats. These protective measures apply to more than 15 percent of the land and 7 percent of Earth's oceans. Organizations such as the National Wildlife Federation, the Wildlife Conservation Society, and the World Wildlife Fund conduct research, raise money, and take action worldwide to protect species.

FACT

Mountain gorillas are found only in Uganda, Rwanda, and the Democratic Republic of the Congo in Africa. Scientists once thought that the mountain gorilla would be extinct by the year 2000. But more than 1,000 now live in the wild as a result of conservation efforts.

In 1973 the U.S. Congress passed the Endangered Species Act to protect critically endangered animal and plant species from extinction. As of 2019, 59 species—including the bald eagle and gray wolf—have recovered and been removed from the endangered species list. Also, 41 other species have been downgraded from endangered to threatened.

CHANGES FOR THE ENDANGERED

In August 2019, President Donald Trump announced changes to the Endangered Species Act (ESA). These changes would allow economic factors such as the revenue from logging or mining to be considered when placing a species on the endangered or threatened list. Also, species on the threatened list would no longer automatically receive the same protections as those on the endangered list. Many environmentalists said that the changes would weaken the law, putting more species at risk.

The changes to the ESA were scheduled to be effective October 2019. However, 17 states, the District of Columbia, and the city of New York filed a lawsuit in September 2019 to block the changes.

Young people around the world led climate strikes on September 13, 2019.

TRANSFORMATIVE CHANGES

Along with all the bad news about Earth, there's also a positive side. If people are capable of great destruction, they're also capable of great acts of positive change. While we tend to be shortsighted, we can also be compassionate.

We humans are dangerous. But we are also problem solvers.

Hope for the Future

U.S. Congress representatives are working on a bill that, if passed, will include rules and plans to make the U.S. economy carbon neutral and promote "economic and environmental justice and equality." Called the Green New Deal, the bill has broad support among American voters and would make a marked difference in efforts to curb biodiversity trends as well as global warming. The U.S. Senate voted against a version of the bill in March 2019, calling it too expensive and ambitious. But lawmakers continue to work on a bill that can pass.

U.S. Representative Alexandria Ocasio-Cortez spoke about the importance of a Green New Deal at a town hall in Washington, D.C., in May 2019.

In April 2019, a group of scientists published a plan to sustain life on Earth. It calls for countries to work together to protect 30 percent of land on Earth and keep it in a natural state by 2030, adding another 20 percent of land as "climate stabilization areas." That doesn't mean that people can't visit these areas. It means that the land can't be used for extracting resources or land conversion. The plan, called the "Global Deal for Nature," specifies how the 30 percent can be reached.

Countries that signed the Convention on Biological Diversity (CBD), a treaty the UN drafted at the first Earth Summit in 1992, have already pledged to preserve 17 percent of land by 2020. But they aren't on pace to meet that goal.

The plan's authors estimate that protecting half of Earth will cost around $100 billion per year. That sounds like a lot of money, but it's available if people are willing. For example, it took less than two days for people to pledge $1 billion to rebuild the Notre Dame Cathedral in France when it burned in 2019. When the U.S. Federal Reserve bailed out banks in 2009, it paid more than $29 trillion. That amount spent to rescue the economy could fund 290 years of conservation efforts that protect half of Earth and stabilize the climate. Nations that belong to the CBD will consider adopting the plan when they meet in 2020.

Acting for Change

People around the world are showing their support for the issue by participating in nonviolent climate protests. On September 20, 2019, about 6 million people participated in nearly 6,000 worldwide climate protests as part of the

Students marched in an Earth Day parade in Vancouver, British Columbia, Canada, on April 22, 2012.

Global Week for Future. Many of the protesters were young people. That week Swedish teenager Greta Thunberg became perhaps the world's most famous climate activist when she attended the United Nations Climate Action Summit in New York City. On September 23, she gave a dramatic speech at the summit, saying through tears that the adults of the world had failed young people by not taking action on climate change. "But the young people are starting to understand your betrayal," she said.

Around the same time as Thunberg's speech, United Nations Secretary General António Guterres said he had started to notice real change by some countries and businesses. For the first time, he said, he felt hopeful that the world could avoid catastrophic heating.

"I see a new momentum," Guterres said, suggesting the world may be at a turning point. "Six months ago, I must tell you, I was quite pessimistic about everything. I would see no movement, now I see a lot of movement and we need to boost that movement."

If what Guterres sees is true, then there is hope. Humans have existed on Earth for 200,000 years, and we have never not had a negative influence on it. The pattern has proven to be extremely hard to stop, even after we should have understood the consequences. It's difficult to fix things—but not too late.

Communities and businesses around the world sponsor tree-planting events to restore the environment.

GRETA THUNBERG

"I don't like being the center of attention," Greta Thunberg has said. "I don't want to be heard all the time, but if there is anything I can do to improve the situation, then I think it's a very small price to pay."

Born and raised in Sweden, Thunberg was eight years old in 2011 when she learned about climate change. She couldn't understand why people weren't doing much about it. She

Greta Thunberg

became depressed, stopped eating, and stopped talking. She was later diagnosed with Asperger's syndrome, a diagnosis she calls her "superpower."

Thunberg wanted to make a difference. She convinced her parents to stop traveling by airplane due to the fuel that flying uses and to stop eating meat because of the toll that raising livestock takes on the environment. In May 2018 she won a climate change essay contest held by a Swedish newspaper. In it, she wrote, "I want to feel safe. How can I feel safe when I know we are in the greatest crisis in human history?"

That August, with Sweden suffering through heat waves and wildfires, Thunberg started her first climate strike. Instead of attending school, she sat across the street from the Swedish legislature every day for three weeks during school hours. She held a sign that read *Skolstrejk för klimatet,* or "school strike for the climate." "The symbolism of the climate strike is that if you adults don't give a damn about my future, I won't either," she said. After the general election that fall, she continued to strike, but only on Fridays. She posted about her strike on social media.

People started to join Thunberg in her protest. Before long, she was speaking before the UN's climate change conference in Poland. Soon she was participating in protests and making speeches all over Europe. In 2019, students throughout the world held climate strikes. Thunberg's protest had grown into a worldwide movement.

When Thunberg came to the United States in August 2019, she didn't travel by airplane. Instead, she sailed in a solar-powered yacht. Besides her speech before the UN Climate Action Summit, she spoke to reporters, appeared on TV, and met with politicians. U.S. Representative Ben Luján of New Mexico asked her, "How can we get more kids involved in this issue?"

"Just tell them the truth," Thunberg replied. "Tell them how it is. Because when I found out how it actually is, it made me furious."

In December 2019, *Time* magazine named Thunberg its Person of the Year. She is the youngest person to ever receive that honor.

Get Involved

It's easy to feel helpless about Earth's condition. What can one person possibly do to end or even slow down the crisis? Meaningful change needs to happen on a huge scale—it's more than one teenager can do.

But there are things you *can* do to take responsibility for your own carbon footprint and raise awareness about this important issue. Even if you're not old enough to vote, you can help influence policy by sharing your views with those in power.

Talk with your family about doing some or all of these things to preserve our planet:

- Help clean and protect parks, reserves, fields, and other areas where wild plants and animals live. If you have a yard, plant native plants that provide habitat and food to native animals. Remove non-native plants.

- Join an organization such as the World Wildlife Fund, the Jane Goodall Institute, the Wildlife Conservation Society, or the Defenders of Wildlife. These organizations use member donations to protect species and habitats.

- Buy certified organic fruits and vegetables at the store or from local growers. Even better, plant a garden to grow and preserve your own organic produce!

- If you own a cat, don't let it roam free outside. In the United States alone, it's estimated that 44 million free-roaming cats kill 4.4 million songbirds every day.

- Be a smart consumer. Buy only things you really need, not just want. Shop for high-quality clothes, shoes, and electronics so you can use them for a long time and then donate them to someone else. When you shop, bring reusable cloth bags for your items instead of using paper or plastic bags from the store.

- Reuse and recycle as much as possible. Buy used items at thrift shops, yard sales, or on internet sites. Many everyday items can be recycled, including aluminum and tin cans, plastic, glass, paper, and cardboard. If you're crafty, consider upcycling—using recycled materials to make both useful and decorative items.

- Eat less meat, especially beef and lamb. If we all eat less meat, the demand will go down. When eating at home or at a restaurant, choose fish that are sustainable. Look for the blue Marine Stewardship Council (MSC) logo.

Carbon Footprint of What You Eat

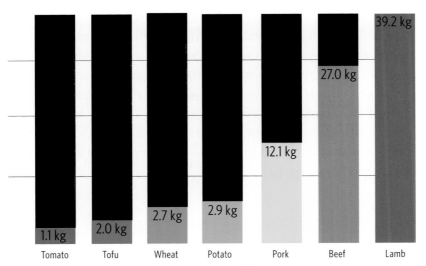

Kilograms of carbon dioxide produced per kilogram of food made

Credit: https://greenmonday.org/environment/

- Transportation is the biggest source of carbon emissions in the United States. Whenever possible, take public transit, bike, or walk instead of using a car.

- Save energy at home. Ask your parents to buy energy-efficient appliances. During winter, turn the thermostat down and put on a sweater or hoodie. During summer, avoid turning on the air conditioning as much as you can. Take showers using lukewarm or cool water and limit them to 10 minutes. Use the cold setting for laundry and dry your clothes on an outdoor line or indoor drying space.

- When traveling, don't buy souvenirs that cost an animal its life, such as items with shells, beaks, fur, bone, or hooves, or items that are taken from the local habitat.

- Encourage adults you know to vote to sustain Earth. Check the policies of candidates at all levels of government and support those who have plans to protect our planet.

Most importantly, stay informed. Keep learning about the science behind the biodiversity crisis and share it with your friends and family. Write, call, or email your local, state or province, and national lawmakers to tell them this issue is important to you. If you need help with what to say, find sample letters online. Search for "climate change advocacy letter" or "climate letter example." You may also want to participate in climate protests near you. Be sure to get permission from your parent or guardian first.

Glossary

biodiversity—the variety of different living species of plants and animals in a given environment

carbon dioxide—a heavy, colorless gas formed by burning fuels, the breakdown or burning of animal and plant matter, and by the act of breathing; it is absorbed from the air by plants in photosynthesis

coral reef—a long line or colony made up of coral, a tiny, soft-bodied animal that lives inside a stony skeleton

ecosystem—the whole group of living and nonliving things that make up an environment and affect each other

fossil fuel—a fuel such as coal, oil, or natural gas that is formed in Earth from plant or animal remains

greenhouse effect—when radiation from the sun is absorbed by Earth and then given off again and absorbed by carbon dioxide and water vapor in the atmosphere, warming the atmosphere

greenhouse gas—a gas such as carbon dioxide or methane that absorbs radiation, traps heat in the atmosphere, and contributes to the greenhouse effect

gross domestic product (GDP)—the total monetary value of all goods and services produced in the country

habitat—the place where an animal or a plant lives and grows in nature

indigenous peoples—ethnic groups who are the original inhabitants of a region

invasive species—a plant or animal species that has been transported from its original habitat into a new habitat where it did not previously exist

poaching—illegal hunting

refugee—a person who flees to a foreign country in order to escape danger

Additional Resources

Critical Thinking Questions

1. Why do you think world leaders have been slow to act and—for the most part—ineffective in combating the biodiversity crisis and climate change?

2. Preventing a sixth great extinction will take a massive effort. What can you do to help? How far are you willing to go? Would you stop eating meat? Or eat less meat? Would you give up air travel?

3. Research invasive species in your area. Why were they moved? What has happened as a result of invasive plants or animals being moved into this new habitat? What is being done to protect native species where you live? How can you help?

Further Reading

Groc, Isabelle. *Gone Is Gone: Wildlife Under Threat*. Victoria, BC: Orca Book Publishers, 2019.

Perdew, Laura. *Biodiversity: Explore the Diversity of Life on Earth with Environmental Science Activities for Kids*. White River Junction, VT: Nomad Press, 2019.

Tavernier, Sarah and Emmanuelle Figueras. *Precious Planet: A User's Manual for Curious Earthlings*. New York: Little Gestalten, 2019.

Thunberg, Greta. *No One Is Too Small to Make a Difference*. New York: Penguin Books, 2019.

Internet Sites

Extinction Rebellion
https://rebellion.earth/

National Geographic
https://www.nationalgeographic.org/

World Wildlife Fund
https://www.worldwildlife.org/

Source Notes

p. 8, "It will be like lots of lights…" Jonathan Watts, "Next Generation 'May Never See the Glory of Coral Reefs,'" *The Guardian,* November 11, 2018, https://www.theguardian.com/environment/2018/nov/11/next-generation-may-never-see-coral-reefs

p. 9, "In five decades we have…" Ibid.

p. 28, "Every morsel of food…" Stephen Leahy, "Half of All Land Must Be Kept in a Natural State to Protect Earth," *National Geographic,* April 19, 2019, https://www.nationalgeographic.com/environment/2019/04/science-study-outlines-30-percent-conservation-2030/

p. 28, "Without them, there is no us…" Ibid.

p. 29, "A billion or more vulnerable…" David Wallace-Wells. *The Uninhabitable Earth: Life After Warming.* New York: Tim Duggan Books, 2019.

p. 30, "There's a saying in the water community…" Ibid.

p. 30, "We are eroding the very foundations…" "Media Release: Nature's Dangerous Decline 'Unprecedented'; Species Extinction Rates 'Accelerating,'" Intergovernmental Science-Policy Platform on Biodiversity and Ecosystem Services (IPBES), May 2019, https://www.ipbes.net/news/Media-Release-Global-Assessment

p. 30, "Global goals for conserving…" Ibid.

p. 43, "The greenhouse effect has been detected…" Andrew Revkin, "Climate Change First Became News 30 Years Ago. Why Haven't We Fixed It?" *National Geographic* magazine, July 2018.

p. 47–48, "Economic and environmental justice…" Naomi Klein, "The Game-Changing Promise of a Green New Deal," *The Intercept,* November 27, 2018, https://theintercept.com/2018/11/27/green-new-deal-congress-climate-change/

p. 50, "But the young people are starting to…" Oliver Milman, "Greta Thunberg Condemns World Leaders in Emotional Speech at UN," *The Guardian,* September 23, 2019, https://www.theguardian.com/environment/2019/sep/23/greta-thunberg-speech-un-2019-address

p. 51, "I see a new momentum…" Oliver Milman, "UN Secretary General Hails 'turning point' in Climate Crisis Fight," *The Guardian,* September 23, 2019, https://www.theguardian.com/world/2019/sep/23/un-secretary-general-antonio-gutteres-turning-point-climate-crisis

p. 52, "I don't like being the center…" Bill Weir, "Greta Thunberg: The Teenage Old Soul of the Climate Crisis," *CNN,* September 20, 2019, https://www.cnn.com/2019/09/20/us/greta-thunberg-profile-weir/index.html

p. 52, "I want to feel safe…" Amelia Tait, "Greta Thunberg: How One Teenager Became the Voice of the Planet," *Wired,* June 6, 2019, https:// www.wired.co.uk/article/greta-thunberg-climate-crisis

p. 53, "The symbolism of the climate…" "Greta Thunberg: The Teenage Old Soul…"

p. 53, "How can we get more kids involved…" Ibid.

p. 53, "Just tell them the truth…" Ibid.

All sites accessed on March 16, 2020.

Select Bibliography

Books

Kolbert, Elizabeth. *The Sixth Extinction: An Unnatural History.* New York: Henry Holt and Company, 2014.

Wallace-Wells, David. *The Uninhabitable Earth: Life After Warming.* New York: Tim Duggan Books, 2019.

Websites and Articles

"The Extinction Crisis," Center for Biological Diversity, Nd., https:// www.biologicaldiversity.org/programs/biodiversity/elements_of_ biodiversity/extinction_crisis/

Flavelle, Christopher, "Climate Change Threatens the World's Food Supply, United Nations Warns," *New York Times,* August 8, 2019, https:// www.nytimes.com/2019/08/08/climate/climate-change-food-supply.ht ml?action=click&module=MoreInSection&pgtype=Article&region=Footer &contentCollection=Climate%20and%20Environment

"How Does Biodiversity Loss Affect Me and Everyone Else?" World Wildlife Fund, Nd., https://wwf.panda.org/our_work/biodiversity/ biodiversity_and_you/

Klein, Naomi, "The Game-Changing Promise of a Green New Deal," *The Intercept,* November 27, 2018, https://theintercept.com/2018/11/27/ green-new-deal-congress-climate-change/

Leahy, Stephen, "Half of All Land Must Be Kept in a Natural State to Protect Earth," *National Geographic,* April 19, 2019, https://www. nationalgeographic.com/environment/2019/04/science-study-outlines- 30-percent-conservation-2030/

Leahy, Stephen, "One Million Species at Risk of Extinction, UN Report Warns," *National Geographic*, May 6, 2019, https://www.nationalgeographic.com/environment/2019/05/ipbes-un-biodiversity-report-warns-one-million-species-at-risk/

"Media Release: Nature's Dangerous Decline 'Unprecedented'; Species Extinction Rates 'Accelerating,'" Intergovernmental Science-Policy Platform on Biodiversity and Ecosystem Services (IPBES), https://www.ipbes.net/news/Media-Release-Global-Assessment

Meyer, Robinson, "The Amazon Cannot Be Recovered Once It's Gone," *The Atlantic*, August 24, 2019, https://www.theatlantic.com/science/archive/2019/08/amazon-fires-are-political/596776/?utm_source=newsletter&utm_medium=email&utm_campaign=atlantic-weekly-newsletter&utm_content=20190825&silverid-ref=MzEwMTU3Mjc5MTcwS0

Milman, Oliver, "Greta Thunberg Condemns World Leaders in Emotional Speech at UN," *The Guardian*, September 23, 2019, https://www.theguardian.com/environment/2019/sep/23/greta-thunberg-speech-un-2019-address

Milman, Oliver, "UN Secretary General Hails 'Turning Point' in Climate Crisis Fight," *The Guardian*, September 23, 2019, https://www.theguardian.com/world/2019/sep/23/un-secretary-general-antonio-gutteres-turning-point-climate-crisis

Plumer, Brad, "Humans Are Speeding Extinction and Altering the Natural World at an 'Unprecedented' Pace," *New York Times*, May 6, 2019, https://www.nytimes.com/2019/05/06/climate/biodiversity-extinction-united-nations.html

Revkin, Andrew, "Climate Change First Became News 30 Years Ago. Why Haven't We Fixed It?" *National Geographic* magazine, July 2018.

Tait, Amelia, "Greta Thunberg: How One Teenager Became the Voice of the Planet," *Wired*, June 6, 2019, https://www.wired.co.uk/article/greta-thunberg-climate-crisis

Victor, David G., Keigo Akimoto, Yoichi Kaya, Mitsutsune Yamaguchi, Danny Cullenward, and Cameron Hepburn, "Prove Paris Was More Than Paper Promises," *Nature*, August 1, 2017, https://www.nature.com/news/prove-paris-was-more-than-paper-promises-1.22378

Watts, Jonathan, "Human Society under Urgent Threat from Loss of Earth's Natural Life," *The Guardian,* May 6, 2019, https://www.theguardian.com/environment/2019/may/06/human-society-under-urgent-threat-loss-earth-natural-life-un-report

Watts, Jonathan, "Next Generation 'May Never See the Glory of Coral Reefs,'" *The Guardian,* November 11, 2018, https://www.theguardian.com/environment/2018/nov/11/next-generation-may-never-see-coral-reefs

Weir, Bill, "Greta Thunberg: The Teenage Old Soul of the Climate Crisis," *CNN,* September 20, 2019, https://www.cnn.com/2019/09/20/us/greta-thunberg-profile-weir/index.html

All sites accessed on March 16, 2020.

About the Author

Eric Braun is the author of books for readers of all ages on topics such as sports, history, current issues, and biographies. He is also a children's book editor and a McKnight Artist Fellow for his fiction. He lives in Minneapolis with his wife, sons, and dog, Willis the Scaredycat.

Index